I0532473

Arranging Words

poems by
Fran Abrams

QUILLKEEPERS PRESS

Copyright © Fran Abrams
Book Cover Design by Quillkeepers Press
Edit by Stephanie Lamb
Format by Quillkeepers Press, LLC

ISBN: 979-8-9891531-1-4

Published by Quillkeepers Press, LLC
PO Box 10236
Casa Grande, AZ 85130

Table of Contents

Arranging Words	1
Performance Review for the Letter A	2
Under the C	3
G gets in our words	4
K Knows How to Hide and Seek	5
O is the letter	6
R Works for Everyone	7
You Have a Friend in T	8
U Is Not Alone	9
Why Oh Y	10
Z is the Loneliest Letter	11
Delicious Words	13
Tastes Like Chocolate	15
School's Out	16
Poetry Exercise	17
Run Fast	18
We Have No Name for Them	19
Negative Capability	20
Words of BLAME	21
Dear Friends	22
Three Little Words	23

Happy as a Lark   25

Beside Myself   26

It Cost an Arm and a Leg   27

Two Left Feet   28

Cold Shoulder   29

She Rubbed Me the Wrong Way   30

All Ears   31

Frog in Her Throat   32

My Last Nerve   33

On the Tip of Your Tongue   34

Cried Her Heart Out   35

In July 2022, the book's title poem, "Arranging Words," was a finalist in the *Prime Number Magazine* Award for Poetry.

Arranging Words

What is the value
of hours spent
coddling words,
coaxing them into
proper order?

Would I do better
to practice sewing,
connecting seams
of blouses and slacks?

Tell me you find solace
when you slip into a poem, find joy
as you button a poem around you.
Then I will continue to favor my pen
over my needle and thread.

Performance Review for the Letter A

You can be angelic at times,
but please try to control your anxiety.
At times, you stand alone
and appear antisocial.

You assist your co-workers
by showing up at the beginning
and in the center of alas and alack.
I fear you overdo yourself in Alabama.

You are an effective member of the team,
helping hold both ends of arena
and arachnophobia, although you needlessly
place yourself in weather and bread.

We appreciate your doing double duty
in aardvark and bazaar. We know
that, on the vowel squad, this job
is usually performed by e and o.

Overall, I must commend you
for acting as the leading letter
of the alphabet and persuading
the other letters to agree.

Under the C

C is the place that hides
craven thoughts,
our crashes and crushes,
a corner where we put our cash.

We won't speak of cruelty,
focus on compassion,
wish for a companion
with whom we're compatible.

We'll appreciate chocolate,
 cookies and cake.
Slip under comforter
when cold makes us chilly.

Under the C is a space
where we care, where
kittens become cats,
and children can climb.

G gets in our words

at the start, the middle, and the end.
Does any other letter go through a bog,
gallop among stags, grip garbage bags?

G is the king who garbles his gossip
while gnawing on bagels and granting
his largesse.

G covers all the angles,
or maybe they're angels
or possibly gryphons.

G is gullible, gracious
and genius. G will be grateful
to get engaged to Gail,
Gianne, or Gabrielle.

K Knows How to Hide and Seek

K knocks twice,
although we hear him only once.

K takes a knee, but no one
knows he's there.

K speaks in skill, but is unheard
in knowledge.

K creaks, cracks, and croaks,
seeks to make people listen,

at times, breaks the bank
and sneaks out the back.

O is the letter

often observed
occupying an opening or
oozing smoothly through schoolroom.

O overcooks omelets,
ogles ospreys,
obeys officers,

objects to oatmeal,
obscures oblivion,
obsesses over odors.

O opposes obedience,
organizes oranges,
outsmarts ogres.

O is an observer
who outgrew obesity,
but not once objectifies
the outcast and ordinary.

R Works for Everyone

R is your friend who's critical of your wardrobe,
your neighbor who tramples your garden.

R is the preacher warning of fire and brimstone,
choir boy whose refrain reaches rafters.

R is the teacher who tries very hard to make algebra
understood.
Principal who reads you the riot act, puts you in the
corner.

R is the driver whose truck fills grocery store racks,
garbage collector who gathers recycling and trash.

R is the burglar and perhaps the murderer
whose crimes are rewarded with prison.

Be careful of R, the versatile letter
who randomly works for everyone.

You Have a Friend in T

Besties with S, you will see T
eating toast and chatting with ghosts.
He is an artist who often paints fast,
who never destroys his thirst.

T doesn't mind following R wearing
a shirt and shorts, although he likes
to take the lead when they travel by train,
always packing a trunk of treats.

T and H together go through thick and thin,
theirs a true friendship they're both thankful for.
You might think they'd be tired of coming in third,
but good friends are known to be tethered.

Sometimes, they might change places,
then T stands after H as is right.
They prefer to eat borscht and not to gain weight
and thought they'd never be caught.

8

U Is Not Alone

U rarely is seen without
another vowel by her side.
She's tough and never stays neutral.
Daughter of a bureaucrat, U requires
a bodyguard. No one can make her eat
cauliflower or do her own laundry.

U flaunts her beauty and aptitude
as entrepreneur. She sells fruit
at her emporium. She drives
an automobile, never a car,
although when courageous,
she may guide a bus.

Her favorite spot is a restaurant
where she loves to eat sauerkraut,
even better if dining in Europe.
She's tasted liqueur and Peruvian soup
and thinks of herself as connoisseur.

She uses a pseudonym as she maneuvers her way
through inscrutable language called English.
She vaults with euphoria, queues for colosseum,
and pauses before saying adieu.

Why Oh Y

Is there any letter of the alphabet
less needed than Y? Do we really
need dairy, or would we all know
what we mean by dairi? Or fairi?
Or canari? After all, we know
how to pronounce spaghetti.

We might find it confusing at first
to pronounce limph, linch or lirics,
and the makers of Lycra and Lysol
might grumble. There's no telling
how the family Smyth might react
if Y's were told to stand back.

The place Y earns recognition is when
it comes at the start of a word. How
would we ever learn to pronounce
yellow, youth, yogurt, and yummy?
That's why we need our beloved Y.
And, yes, we keep Y on hand
for our prayers.

Z is the Loneliest Letter

Z is the least used letter in English
we're told. It's razzle and dazzle,
but where do you use it every day?
Perhaps you visit the zoo or play the zither?

Are you organized? Or frenzied?
Maybe you're a wizard or a lover
of zucchini. I'm sure pizza
is not far from your thoughts.

You may need a zipper, but
I hope you have no use
for an embezzler and don't need
to exorcize any demons.

You may walk on terrazzo,
add garbanzo beans to salad,
schmooze with your neighbors,
and memorize phone numbers.

You might walk around in a daze,
take time to read a magazine,
agonize over what to cook for dinner,
then take something from the freezer.

You should avoid hazards,
but like to play puzzles,
and a steak that is sizzling
has zing with a pretzel.

And look, I've already
written six stanzas
using the loneliest letter
that always amazes.

Delicious Words

Try some words
that are delightfully tasty:
Ukulele
Omnivorous
Maximize

Chewing on words is good for digestion,
but set aside difficult words
that must be sounded out
for when there's time
to enjoy a leisurely lunch.

Savor the fine wine
of classic words:
The woods are lovely, dark and deep,
While I nodded, nearly napping, suddenly there
came a tapping
When the evening is spread out against the sky

For variety, try words
that taste like sounds:
Slurp
Beep
Dribble

Cleanse your palate
with words that are crisp:
Snack
Brittle
Peppermint

Quoted lines are from:

"Stopping By Woods On A Snowy Evening -
Stopping By Woods On A Snowy Evening."
PoemHunter.Com, 13 June 2016,
www.poemhunter.com/poem/stopping-by-woods-on-
a-snowy-evening-2/.

Poe, Edgar Allan. "The Raven by Edgar Allan Poe."
Poetry Foundation, Poetry Foundation,
www.poetryfoundation.org/poems/48860/the-raven.
Accessed 19 Sept. 2023.

Eliot, T. S. "The Love Song of J. Alfred Prufrock by
T. S. Eliot." *Poetry Foundation*, Poetry Foundation,
www.poetryfoundation.org/poetrymagazine/poems/44
212/the-love-song-of-j-alfred-prufrock. Accessed 19
Sept. 2023.

Tastes Like Chocolate

I have always wanted to offer you a poem
that tastes like chocolate. The words will melt
on your tongue so you can savor the sweet sensation
on your taste buds, enjoy each delectable word.

I have always wanted a recipe that puts my poem
in the same class as the world's best brownie.
Words in your mouth releasing
chocolate flavor that makes you swoon.

If I knew the ingredients for a poem
that tastes like chocolate, I would present
my poem to those who insist,
I've never understood poetry.

A collection of poems that taste like chocolate
might tempt more people to enjoy
a morsel of insight, a reminder of sweetness,
a serving of comfort.

School's Out

Golden Shovel for Reuben Jackson

It was the last day of school. We
cleaned out our lockers and danced
in the hallways, did a hop and skip as
we rushed to where the bus waited, the driver well
prepared for the chaos about to board as
she pulled the lever to open the door. Our
home-bound bodies stepped up, carrying the cumbersome
remains of the school year—forgotten assignments, boots
left in school all those months since cold weather would
require them, all the debris our book bags would allow.

Poetry Exercise

Brain cells stretch,
lift your arms,
reach for words.

Tell me cells, how
would you express joy?
Bounce on your toes.
Move and make it rhyme.

You over there,
third cell from the left,
Drop, and give me
three synonyms for sunshine.

Lift your legs, cells.
Let's kick up the rhythm.
I want to see you jump
and work the line.

Run Fast

Golden Shovel for Ann Quinn

I am running after you
as you ride your two-wheeler, although I have
no chance of running fast enough to
keep up, a lesson I refuse to learn
as I try to catch my breath, to
run like Superman, to go
faster than a speeding bullet fired against
the wall, a stray bullet we all
run from—reacting from experience, from instinct.

We Have No Name for Them

When both your parents have died,
whether you are six or 25 or 64,
you are an orphan.

When a wife loses her spouse,
she is called widow.
A husband, after losing wife,
is known as widower.

When a parent loses a child,
we have no name for that.
When a boy loses his sister,
there is no word to label him.

Whether his sister died a victim
of car crash, shooting, or illness,
we have no vocabulary
for those who remain.

The only word that comes to mind—survivor,
as in—she is survived by her parents and her brother,
whose lives have been forever shattered by her loss.

We have no name to wrap around them.

Negative Capability

Neither of us had ever
Experienced a sight as
Grand as this before
A wide panorama revealing ancient
Tiers of stone
Igneous rock stacked
Vertically over centuries until
Eventually rivers wore through it forming

Canyons
Adorned with layers of color
Patterns laid one
Atop another, rough surfaces dotted with small trees and
Bushes surviving
In harsh environment where
Living things take nutrients from
Inhospitable places by sending
Their roots deep into rocky soil just as
You succeed even when not expected to

Words of BLAME

There is no use assigning BLAME.
It's a meager MEAL at best.
Some might say a sacrificial LAMB.

BLAME stands in for anger,
ABLE to make your thoughts
futile as well as LAME.

You can sit under an ELM,
AMBLE down a road,
and find that to be a BALM

more comforting than BLAME.
These words are not proven in a LAB,
and go down better with a mug of ALE.

Dear Friends

if sad, read rare ideas
raid den and diner
defend fried ferns
and seared sardine

desire defies fear
dreads rain and
air near sea reefs
siren raised refrain

resin freed red fire
rinsed, sanded, safe
rinds snared rare deer
ferries eased firs

eraser denies fair reader
defines rarified deeds
drains dense dead sea
infers sadder needs

Three Little Words

Seize the day
Now or never
Be the change

Every vote counts
Winners never quit
Believe in yourself

Look both ways
Never look back
Wash your hands

Count your blessings
Find your passion
Dare to dream

Knowledge is power
Just do it
Nothing is impossible

Follow your heart
Dreams come true
Love conquers all

Family is forever
Call your mother
Handle with care

Do not bend
This side up
Refrigerate after opening

Live and learn
Forgive and forget
Lifeguard on duty

Happy as a Lark

It's not easy finding
the bluebird of happiness.
Some are more likely to find
themselves called crazy as a loon.
Others shed problems
like water off a duck's back.

When birds of a feather
flock together, bad times
are as scarce as hen's teeth.
You've seen them, looking
proud as a peacock,
flying high, free as a bird.

Beside Myself

Here I stand beside myself,
trying to see myself through
the eyes of another, knowing
the eyes still are mine.

Standing beside myself,
I feel detached from my emotions.
Was I not recently beside myself
with joy? Why can I not recall

those feelings now? And earlier,
I am sure I was beside myself
with grief. Whose numbness
was that? Was it only a facade?

Am I myself or the one
beside myself?

It Cost an Arm and a Leg

She collected mannequins.
Some only torsos or arms or legs.
Arms straight or flexed at the elbow
if designed to carry a bag.

Heads were difficult to find.
So many shops used
mannequins without them.
Her collection took over

her living room, dining room
and spare bedroom. Moving
around her house, she
encountered arms or legs

in awkward positions,
some knees bent, as if
trying to escape.

She worked extra hours
at her day job to support
the cost of arms and legs.

Two Left Feet

Do you know how expensive it is
to buy shoes when you have
two left feet? The only way
to acquire shoes is to buy
two pair of the same design
and wear only the left ones.

I keep looking for someone
with two right feet who likes
my taste in shoes
and wants my extras.

Do you realize how difficult it is
to take dance lessons? The teacher
stands in front of the class and repeats
left, right, left, right, or left, left, right, right.
No matter the instructions, I find my legs
tangled around each other.

I keep looking for someone
with two right feet who will
dance with me and not trip
over my two left feet.

Cold Shoulder

Shirley was never warm enough.
Always complained about her left shoulder.
Cold, she said through shivering teeth.
Even my sweater won't keep me warm.

One day Janice said something offensive
about Shirley's work, something simple,
like it was always messy. Shirley decided
to give Janice the cold shoulder.

What a relief. Now Shirley is always
warm enough and Janice constantly
begs to have the heat turned up.

She Rubbed Me the Wrong Way

She insisted on stroking my cheek
from my chin to my eyebrow
instead of the other way around.

She knew I didn't like to have my head
rubbed, as it made me feel as if
a headache was coming on.

And when I asked her to rub ointment
on my wounds, she rubbed it all
over my arms. She told me, sadly,
she never learned how to rub the right way.

All Ears

She had a reputation
for being a good listener.
What her friends
didn't know is that she had

ears all over her head. She
was grateful for her thick,
curly auburn hair that hid
her numerous ears from all

but the most intrusive viewer.
Still, whenever someone said to her,
I'm all ears to mean they
were paying close attention,

she was always tempted to answer,
If you only knew.

Frog in Her Throat

She had heard that, if
you weren't careful, tree frogs
would leap into your mouth
thinking it a moist, warm place

to hide. Now here she was,
with a frog lodged in her throat,
and no obvious way to remove it.
Some tree frogs, she knew,

made a sound like barking,
and so, she tried to bark.
She produced a sound much like
a seal's bark. The tiny frog

leapt out of her throat
and began a frenzied search
for the male frog who
had barked that mating call.

My Last Nerve

My store is not remarkable.
Front windows display
images of fearless people,
not fancy hats or handmade bowls.

Inside, it's all display boards
listing what's in stock:
    Nerve to face an unfaithful spouse
    Nerve to bungee jump
    Nerve to stand up to a rude boss
    Nerve to try a new haircut

It's a successful business.
People need nerve these days.
The most popular, such as
nerve to propose marriage,
sell quickly.

At holiday times,
I sometimes sell out.
You can imagine my shock
when someone
got on my last nerve
without paying.

On the Tip of Your Tongue

I have observed people recently
who have pierced
their tongues, adorned
the tip with a silver ball or ring.

It's mesmerizing,
difficult to look away
when you talk to them,
silver jewelry bobbing.

It worries me when they
pierce their tongues.
Let's not forget where
unremembered words reside.
I hope silver doesn't
block memory's path.

Cried Her Heart Out

She sat, wiping her face
with tissues, considering
her feelings of grief

and disbelief upon learning
her friend had killed himself.
She cried and cried

until she found her heart
in her hands and realized
she had cried her heart out.

How grateful she was
she had caught it
before it hit the floor.

Fran Abrams lives in Rockville, MD. She holds an undergraduate degree in art and architecture and a master's degree in urban planning. For 41 years, she worked in government and nonprofit agencies in Montgomery County, MD, where her work included a significant amount of writing, such as legislation, regulations, guidelines, grant proposals, reports, and other bureaucratic necessities.

In addition to her day job, she began working in 2000 as a visual artist. After retiring in 2010, she devoted much of her time to her art. In 2016, she wrote a lengthy funding proposal to support Foundry

37

Gallery, a nonprofit art gallery in Washington, DC, where she exhibited her artwork. After completing that proposal, she realized how much she missed expressing herself in words.

Fran decided she wanted to write in a form that was completely different from her past work. She attended a poetry reading early in 2017, and, inspired by that experience, she began taking poetry writing classes at The Writer's Center in Bethesda, MD. In September 2017, she traveled to Italy with her first writing instructor and a group of women poets for a poetry retreat that reinforced her commitment to writing poems. She continues to take classes about the craft of writing poetry.

Fran's poems have been published online and in print in *Cathexis-Northwest Press*, *The American Journal of Poetry*, *MacQueen's Quinterly Literary Magazine*, *The Ravens Perch*, *Gargoyle*, and many others. Her poems appear in more than a dozen anthologies, including the 2021 collection titled *This is What America Looks Like* from Washington Writers Publishing House (WWPH).

In December 2021, she won the WWPH Winter Poetry Prize for her poem titled "Waiting for Snow." In July 2022, her poem "Arranging Words" was a finalist in the 2022 *Prime Number Magazine* Award for Poetry.

In 2019, she was a juried poet at Houston (TX) Poetry Fest. She was a featured reader at DiVerse

Gaithersburg (MD) Poetry Reading in 2021 and 2023. In January 2023, she was a guest author on the podcast *Quintessential Listening: Poetry Online Radio* hosted by Dr. Michael Anthony Ingram. She read at the Kensington, MD, Day of the Book Festival in April 2023, and the Gaithersburg, MD, Book Festival in May 2023.

Her autobiographical book of poems titled *I Rode the Second Wave: A Feminist Memoir* was published in 2022 by Atmosphere Press. In April 2023, her first chapbook, titled *The Poet Who Loves Pythagoras*, was published by Finishing Line Press.

Please visit www.franabramspoetry.com for more.